Make My Own Living Trust

E. J. Lashlee

Make My Own Living Trust. Copyright 2012 E. J. Lashlee

Copyright 2012 E.J. Lashlee. All rights reserved.
ISBN 978-1-105-76648-0

THANK YOU

I have had guidance, training, experience, support, and advice from so many over the years.

Some of the most important people are Kris Farrell, Dennis Richard, Tom Wiesner, Hal, Darrell Clark, Gary, Joe, Mace Gazda, Uncle Dan, Mark Miscevic, Carol, Homer Black, Robert, Randy, Lou Baldelli, Ed Solomon, Aunt Opal, Lou Senter, Al, John, Scott Brown, Cindy, Laurie, and of course..... my brothers, my sister, my kids, my mom and dad, and my wife.

Contents

Page 1   Reasons for Trusts
              Best Known Types of Trusts

Page 3   A Diagram: Protected vs. Unprotected Assets

Page 5   Lifetime Benefits

Page 7   Inheritance Descendant Chart

Page 9   Make Your Own Living Trust

Page 27 Instructions

REASONS FOR TRUSTS

Manage Assets
Protect Children
Protect Grandchildren
Protect Wife
Protect from child's wife or husband
Protect from child's mistakes or legal entanglements
Protect Parents
Protect Business
Protect from loss of house
Provide for School
Provide for Health
Provide for Education
Provide for unable persons
Provide for minors until of age
Provide for minors until education
Provide for minors until married
Protect from potential FUTURE debts
Separate assets into Separate assets that are not guaranteeing each other
Provide management of income to restricted persons such as:
    Citizens without income
    Citizens with income limits for retirement
    Citizens with income for medical benefits
    Citizens with income for state aid benefits
Eliminate death taxes
Provide for tax savings
Shift taxes to a specific person or persons
Provide tax bracket lowering
Eliminate double taxation such as corporation or partnership taxes
Protect from potential FUTURE tax debts
Eliminate probate

> A Trust can accomplish many of these solutions within the same document.

> Any Trust can be more than one type of Trust

BEST KNOWN TYPES OF TRUSTS

Living Revocable Trust
Family Trust
Contract of Trust
Statutory Trust or trust by Statute
Settlor Trust
Simple Trust
Creator Trust
Grantor Trust
Crummey Trust
Insurance Trust
Inter Vivos Trust
Verbal Trust
Testamentary Trust
Generation-Skipping Trust
Spendthrift Trust
A/B Trust
A/B/C Trust
Pourover Trust
Remainder Trust
Foreign Trust
Custom Trust

Q-Tip Trust
G.R.A.T. Trust
G.R.I.T. Trust
Reit Trust
Trust by Will
Family Limited Trust
Personal Residence Trust
Stock Holding Trust
Passive Trust
Blind Trust
U.B.O.
Business Trust
Land Trust
Illinois Land Trust
Massachusetts Trust
Deed of Trust
Trust Deed
Investment Trust
Corporate Trust
Banking Trust
Children's Trust

Public Trust
Charitable Trust
Court Trust
Anti-Stalking Trust
Charitable Remainder Trust
Uni-Trust
Asset Protection Trust
Privacy Trust

> All Trusts created by a person while still alive are defined as "LIVING TRUSTS"

> Any Trust can be either Revocable or Irrevocable

Make My Own Living Trust. Copyright 2012 E. J. Lashlee

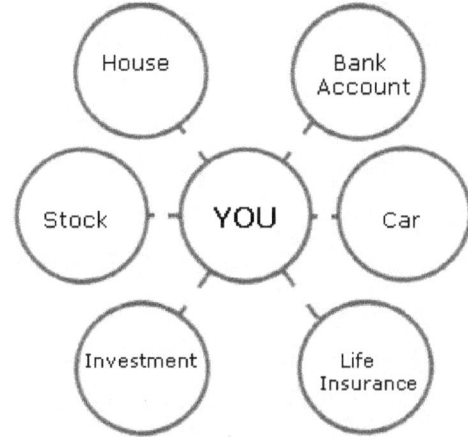

1. **Trust vs. Corporation:** Trust is better – No public disclosure or personal liability of controlling parties – Complete and total separation of business and personal assets – No double taxation on business income – No corporate renewal or usage fees – Can operate freely in all 50 states.

2. **Asset Protection:** Assets are held in totally separate Trusts that are answerable solely unto themselves. You retain all benefits of control without the liabilities involved with having assets titled to your name.

3. **Privacy:** Controlling parties of Trust assets are not known to anyone unless you tell them. There is no need for off shore bank accounts. You can manage the funds of a Trust account at the bank next door in complete privacy.

4. **Lawsuit Protection:** Most Attorneys will file a significant financial suit against you only after verifying that they will be able to collect on a judgment. Assets held in a Private Asset Trust are not yours. As long as assets are properly managed and the transfer into Trust was not a fraudulent conveyance to avoid a pre-existing debt, Trust assets cannot be attached to satisfy a personal judgment claim.

5. **Access to Funds:** A Court can freeze your personal and business assets, pending the outcome of a case against you, whether you are right or wrong. Assets owned by a Private Asset Trust are not associated with an attachment or restraining order aimed at your assets.

6. **Negotiations Leverage:** An Asset Protection Program, utilizing Private Asset trusts, moves the negotiating chips to your side of the table. It gives you the power to dictate the terms of any settlement.

7. **Tax Sheltering:** Dividend income received from a Trust is not subject to Self Employment Tax – Managing Dividend dispersal from a Trust allows for income shifting among several beneficiaries to control individual tax brackets – Income that is generated and maintained by a Trust that is domiciled in a tax free state or district is not subject to state income tax.

8. **Estate Tax Savings:** A Private Asset Trust program will allow you to reduce the size of your taxable estate – with no loss of control – and reduce or eliminate estate taxes.

9. **Probate Fees:** No Probate – all assets transfer to your heirs according to your instructions.

10. **Revocable Living Trust:** Gives you none of the above benefits other than limited Estate Tax Savings and avoidance of Probate. Much less protective or private than a Private Asset Trust Structure.

LIFETIME BENEFITS	With a Will	Corporation Or LLC	Living Trust	Private Asset Trust
Buy, Sell, Loan, Borrow or Pledge Assets	Normal	Officer Must Sign	Trustee Must Sign	Trustee Must Sign
Flexibility to Do as You Want	Normal	Shareholders Must Approve	Yes, Sometimes	Yes
Maintain Privacy of Benefits	No	Seldom	Sometimes	Yes
Maintain Privacy of Control	No	No	No	Yes
Separate and Protect Individual Assets	No	Sometimes	No	Yes
Establish Credit Separate from Personal Credit	No	Sometimes	No	Sometimes
Separate Business and Personal Affairs	No	Sometimes	No	Yes
Limit State & Federal Taxes	No	Sometimes	No	Yes
Limit Self-Employment Taxes	No	No	No	Yes
Limit Lawsuit Liability	No	Sometimes	No	Yes
Change Beneficiary Interests as Desired	N/A	No	Sometimes	Yes
Allow for Private and Government Health Care	No	No	Sometimes	Yes
Earn Income Without Affecting Social Security	No	No	No	Sometimes
Documentation and Accounting Requirements	Normal	Extensive	Normal	Normal
Annual Reporting & Fees	No	Yes	No	No
Valid in Multiple States	Sometimes	No, Unless Each State Paid	Sometimes	Yes
Startup Costs	Minor	High if Properly Organized	About 1/2 of a Corporation	About Same as Corporation
Annual Costs	Minor	High if Properly Organized	Minor	Minor
Difficulty of Management	Minor	Medium if Properly Maintained	Minor	Minor

Inheritance Descendant Chart

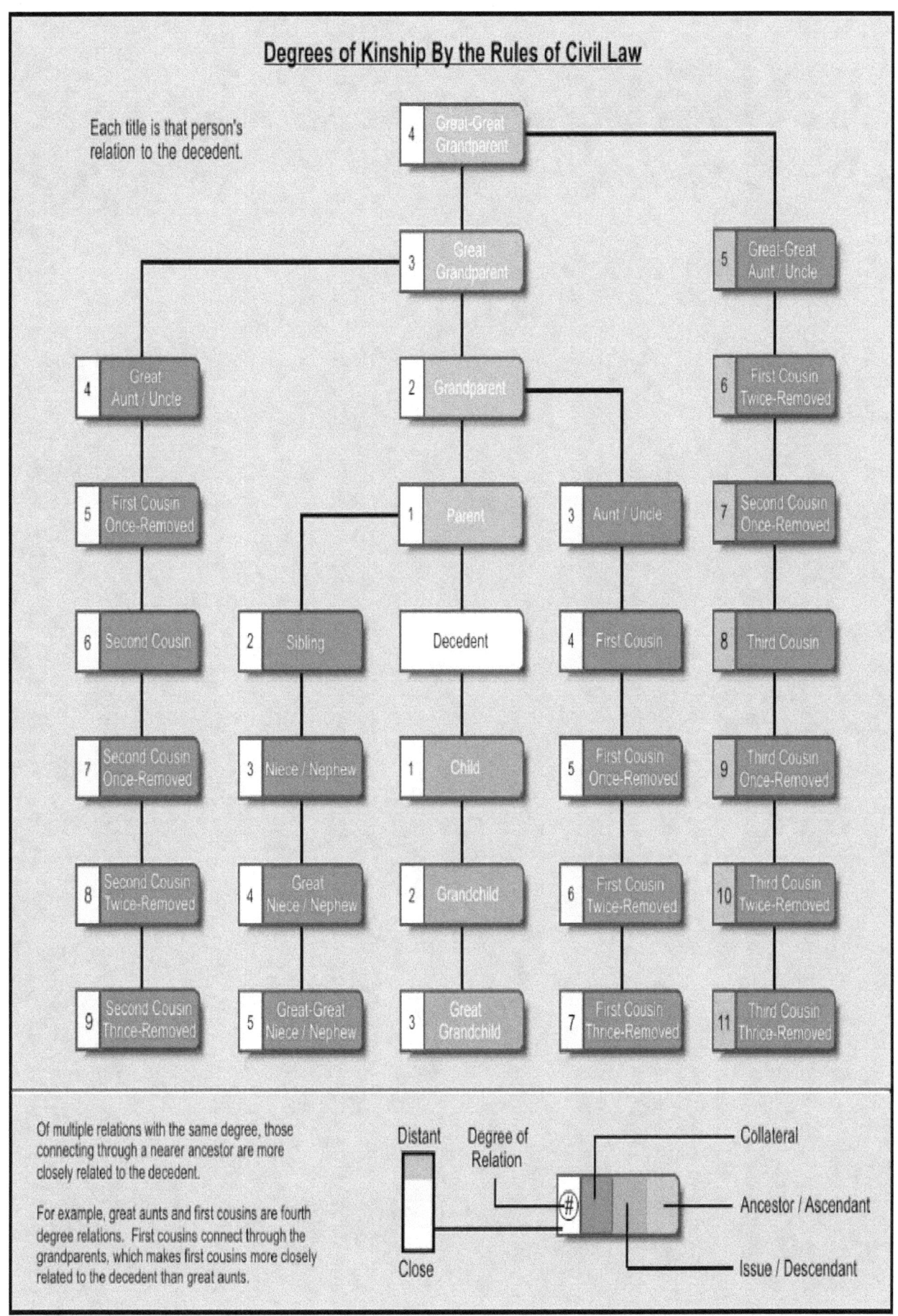

LIVING TRUST

(Cover Sheet, Description, and Disclaimer)

The attached LIVING TRUST hereby accepts ownership of various assets secured for the beneficiaries.

The name of this Living Trust is:

_____

This is a private Living Trust agreement with private registration.

This Living Trust takes effect and is certified by the VERIFIED SEAL of Guardian Guaranty Group upon witnessed and/or notarized SIGNATURE which is then registered with www.TrustRegistry.net for the trust.

This is not insurance or a Policy of Insurance. This is not an insurance agreement or involved with securities, stock, investing, investments, services, or other products. None of the parties to this agreement are a government agency. Nothing in this agreement is offered by a insurance company, securities company, or government agency. Parties to this agreement will not disclose, sell, trade, or lend information to anyone other than the herein included and signed parties.

I/We have received and understand this Description and Disclaimer, and hereby agree and participate in this agreement for the benefit of the beneficiaries.

_____ Dated _____

_____, Trustee
(applicant signature)

LIVING TRUST - Worksheet

Trust Title: _____ (Select a Trust Name with 28 character max)

(BEST is to use INITIALS / Try NOT to use NAMES of persons / BEST to use "TRUST" as the last word in title)

(EXAMPLE:"A. B. SMITH TRUST"=17 characters)

1. The name(s) of CREATOR(s) is/are: _____;

    (only ONE is required)

2. The name(s) of CURRENT TRUSTEE(s) is/are: (Person "IN CHARGE" with all powers)

    Trustees: _____, _____; (only ONE is required)

3. The name(s) of the CURRENTLY SUCCESSOR TRUSTEE(S) is/are: (Backup Person "IN CHARGE" with all powers)

    Successor Trustees: _____, _____; (only ONE is required)

4. The name(s) of BENEFICIARIES:

    _____, _____,
    _____, _____,
    _____, _____,
    _____, _____,
    _____, _____; (any number is OK, or just indicate "SAME AS X")

5. The number of trustees that must sign documents is [_] ONE [_] TWO.

ASSETS TO INCLUDE:	Account Number	Approx. Value	Approx. Debt	Comments

To REGISTER, Make check payable to: "REGISTRY", then deliver a copy of the original completed and signed agreement, together with the exact registration fee of $19.00 to:

REGISTRY
c/o Trustee
668 N. PCH #400
Laguna Beach, CA 92651

Phone (347) 687-2878

Email: info@TrueTrustServices.com

Payment by:_____ Date:_____
_____

Clerk

LIVING TRUST

This Living Trust Agreement replaces and supersedes all previous agreements, if any, and is made between the undersigned signatories as a beneficial arrangement NAMED:

_____

1. TRUST PROPERTY. The Trustee hereby accepts assignments, exchanges,

   and transfers to the Trust of all of the following equities, assignments, designs, awards, bank assets, contracts, agreements, inheritances, judgments, investments, stock, bonds, equipment, inventory, cash, vehicles, insurance, real property, personal property, collectables, recoveries, income, refunds, products, gifts, royalties, dividends, bills of sale, trade names, creations, patents, copyrights, trademarks, partnerships, or additional declared assets.

   Additional Item to Include:

ASSETS TO INCLUDE:	Account Number	Approx. Value	Approx. Debt	Comments

   Other assigned assets may be accepted or declared from time-to-time by

   written or oral declaration, or recorded title change and shall be considered

   accepted when registered with TrustRegistry.net for the trust.

2. TRUSTEE POWERS. The Trustee shall have the following powers:

   (a) To buy, sell, hold, convey, encumber, rent, declare, repair, destroy,
       improve, deduct, retain, expend, pay out, incur expenses, report, invest, lease any property, money, or value of the Trust, or any additional property which may be received by the Trustee, whether or not income producing, as is deemed appropriate by the Trustee;

   (b) To borrow or lend money for any purpose, and/or to secure the repayment by note, mortgage, trust deed, contract, interest in, security, pledge, joint venture, partner, or encumber the Trust;

   (c) To freely act under all or any of the powers of this Agreement in

all matters concerning the Trust, by personal honor and without the necessity of obtaining the consent or permission of any interested person or of any court. The powers granted to the Trustee may be exercised in whole or in part, and shall be supplementary to and not exclusive of the general powers of a trustee pursuant to law, and shall include all powers necessary to carry them into effect;

(d) trustee may uniquely divide, combined, split, assign, obligate, distribute, benefit, distribute, retain, report, disclose, or pay others to include debtors, taxes, debts, trustees, or beneficiaries;

at the sole discretion of the trustee.

(e) Creator [_] or Trustee, may alter, amend, or revoke the Trust.

PAGE 1

3. TRUSTEES. Additionally, the following are named as Trustees:

Trustee: _____

Trustee: _____

4. BENEFICIARIES. No title to any of the Trust assets shall vest in any Beneficiary until the actual termination of this Trust. Undivided beneficial interest shall [_] distributed, [_] held in trust for:

Beneficiary: _____ of ____%
Beneficiary: _____ of ____%
Beneficiary: _____ of ____%
Beneficiary: _____ of ____%
Beneficiary: _____ of ____%
Beneficiary: _____ of ____%
Beneficiary: _____ of ____%

5. BOND. No Trustee shall give any bond or other security.

6. REVOCABILITY. This Trust is revocable, and the Settlor does not waive all rights and powers, whether individually or in conjunction with others, and regardless of when or from what source he may have acquired such rights or powers, to alter, amend, revoke, or terminate the Trust.

7. TERM. The term of this Trust is [_] Twenty-one years from this date, [_] Life of Creator plus twenty-one years.

8. JURISDICTION AND LAW. This Living Trust has been executed under the Laws of

[_] The state of _____ [_] all territories and the United States.

Dated _____

_____
Creator

_____
Trustee

[SEAL: Guardian Guaranty Group, Organized 1977, United States of America]

Accepted per SEAL affixed hereto by
Guardian Guaranty Group, Protector

_____
(witness)

_____
(witness)

Copyright © www.TrueTrustServices.com   Phone: (347) 687-2878   PAGE 2

____SPACE ABOVE THIS LINE FOR RECORDER USE_____

(Registration Cover Sheet)

CERTIFICATION OF TRUST

See Attached **"CERTIFICATION OF TRUST"** for the **LIVING TRUST**

REQUEST FOR NOTICE to:

Postal MAIL:
REGISTRY
c/o Trustee
668 N. PCH #400 LB, CA 92651
Email: info@TrueTrustServices.com
Attn: Registration

RECORDED by & MAIL to: _____

CERTIFICATION OF TRUST

The trust known as **LIVING TRUST,** executed on _____ is a valid and existing trust, Registration #_____.

The undersigned declare(s) under penalty of perjury that the following is true and correct.

1. The name(s) of the CREATOR is/are: _____;

2. The name(s) of the CURRENTLY ACTING TRUSTEE(S) is/are:
   Trustees: _____;
   Trustees: _____;

3. The name(s) of the SUCCESSOR TRUSTEE(S) is/are:
   Successor Trustee: _____;

4. The name(s) of BENEFICIARIES:
   _____,
   _____,
   _____,
   _____,
   _____,
   _____,

5. Each herein named Trustee is qualified to act on behalf of the Trust. Trustee is authorized to act for any asset, do banking, check, stock, real estate, escrow, insurance, or other action. The Trustee may buy, sell, hold, convey, encumber, rent, borrow, lend, secure, mortgage, contract, share, pledge, encumber, report, repair, destroy, improve, deduct, retain, insure, expend, pay out, incur expenses, invest, lease, compromise, settle, arbitrate, sign, agree, negotiate, defend, contract, claim, demand, protect, as Trustee, or act through an agent or attorney-in-fact without obtaining the consent of any person or court.

6. The Trust is [_] irrevocable   [_] revocable by _____.

7. The number of trustees that must sign documents is [_] ONE [_] TWO.

8. Guardian Guaranty Group is registered as Protector and Arbitrator with TrustRegistry.net by private recording with exclusive absolute power to appoint, define, and clarify the trust, and to settle disputes between and for all parties to the trust. Protector shall maintain a copy of the trust.

9. The Trust has not been revoked, modified, or amended in any manner which would cause the representations contained herein to be incorrect.

Each of us declares under penalty of perjury under the laws of the United States of America that the herein signatories signed this document in our presence, all of us being present at the same time, and we now sign below declaring that the signatories appear to be of sane mind and under no duress, fraud or undue influence.

_____

Trustee

_____

_____

(witness)

Copyright © www.TrueTrustServices.com   Phone: (347) 687-2878

INSTRUCTIONS

Make My Own Family Trust With Forms & Support

What is a trust?

A Living Trust is where you place ownership of assets into a Contract (controlled by yourself) to be given later to someone else, after you are pass on. During your life, you retain full control and can modify, amend, or cancel the trust.

Who can be the creator?

Anyone that is a legal person and that is NOT controlled by guardians or a court such as Bankruptcy Court.

Who can be the beneficiary?

Anyone, (usually your relatives). During your life, you retain full benefit, use, and control; unless you determine otherwise.

Is a Notary required?

Most states and companies will accept two Witnesses instead of a Notary. Witnesses may be (or not) a party named in the trust agreement. Notarized signatures may be required by some companies or states, and a Notary eliminates the need for Witnesses.

How do I/we transfer assets?
- A) A) Go to the bank with your completed Living Trust and have them change the title to bank accounts to be in the name of your trust.
- B) On your home, you will need to create a transfer by Deed. Contact our support team for assistance, or we can prepare a Deed for you.
- C) On your cars and boats and motorcycles. The Motor Vehicle Department will probably want to see proof of your completed trust, and will then assist you in transfers to your trust.
- D) Hobby collectables, jewelry, guns, tools, electronics, furniture, coins, and other personal items can be transferred by a written Bill of Sale, Transfer Agreement, Gift, or just listed in the Living Trust. Details and descriptions can be written, photographed, or a video can be made.

What about maintaining insurance?

Insurance companies can be notified to add the Living Trust as an "additional insured" or you can reverse it and name the Living Trust as the "primary insured", with yourself as additional insured. The cost is minimal or additions are free, depending on the company.

Why should I get the trust privately registered?

Registering the Living Trust provides for privacy from outsiders, yet verifies that the trust exists after you pass on, and keeps unwanted individuals from viewing, destroying, or modifying your trust. The TrustRegistry.net company also holds backup copies, and will keep your amendments, copied photographs, videos, and Statement of Wishes safely as well. You can also keep the details private from the beneficiaries until they are activated, to keep family relations under control. This can be the best method to allow for further modifications without conflict.

How do I/we make changes later?

Simply create a page on your computer called "AMENDMENT to the _____ Trust". Then declare your modifications, and sign it in front of a Notary, or we can prepare a the document for you.

About the Included Forms:

1) LIVING TRUST – Just a Cover Sheet, Description, and Disclaimer – optional

2) PRIVATE LIVING TRUST – Worksheet – Just a simple practice worksheet – optional

3) LIVING TRUST – 2 pages – This is the actual LIVING TRUST AGREEMENT DOCUMENT

4) Registration Cover Sheet – For "CERTIFICATION OF TRUST" page

5) CERTIFICATION OF TRUST – A Mini-Info Sheet that some banks require (or that can be shown) instead of showing the complete trust (Item 3 above).

Here is our Free National Support Phone: (347) 687-2878 and Email: info@TrueTrustServices.com

BONUS:

Free 10 Minute Phone Consultation available by your email request. Please prove your phone number and best times to call back.

Copyright © www.TrueTrustServices.com   Phone: (347) 687-2878

www.ingramcontent.com/pod-product-compliance
Lightning Source LLC
Chambersburg PA
CBHW080855170526
45158CB00009B/2741